This book is dedicated to my children. I wouldn't be where I am without any of you.

To Dre, you've always lived life fearlessly. That's one of the things that I have always loved about you. Never allow anyone to dim that in you, use that for the kingdom of Christ. Alym, my sweet boy. Life and people will try to break you. They will see that you have an amazing heart, but remember to protect/guard that. Remember what the bible says about that. Poppa. my baby boy! You are my sunshine, my little sunshine. You are a person of few words, but your actions says it all.
Mama, Miss Rosie... my only baby girl, you gave my life meaning again after losing your uncle. I love you more than you know sweet girl. Keep pushing your brothers to their full potential.
God has no limits and neither do any of you.
-Mama

Dear reader, first I would like to say thank you. Thank you for choosing to read, learn, and understand, who Christ has called you to be through who am I? Who did God say that I am? You could have chosen any other devotional, but you are here. I pray this book affirms and confirms everything you have been praying for. I pray these scriptures are even confirmation of what God has already said to you and about you.

"The Lord bless you and keep you; the Lord make his face shine on you and be gracious toward you and give you peace."
-Numbers 6:24-26 (NIV)

I remember thinking that I could do it all alone. That I could disconnect myself from the source of life and handle my affairs on my own. Then God reminded me of John 15:1-5 and I remembered that without Christ I am nothing and can't accomplish anything. It is the connection with Christ and through him that makes it possible that I can do all things.

WHO DID GOD SAY I AM?

"I am the true grapevie, and my Father is the gardener. Yes, I am the vine; you are the branches. Those who remain in me, and I in them, will produce much fruit. For apart from me you can do nothing."

John 15:1, 5 (NLT)

GOD SAYS

Have you ever met someone and they loved you so much so that you had to ask why? Whenever I think of the goodness of Christ and all he has done for me, I am reminded that I am a child of God!

WHO AM I THAT YOU WERE THINKING OF ME?

"But to all who have believed him and accepted him, he gave the rights to become children of God."

John 1:12 (NLT)

GOD SAYS

Who the son sets free, is free indeed. I am not sure if anyone feels this way, but to have a friend, a good friend, a genuine friend is beyond what words can express. To have a friend die for you, now that's life-changing. Because of the death of Christ and his resurrection, I am free!

I AM FREE!

"I no longer call you slaves, because a master doesn't confide in his slaves. Now you are my friends, since I have told you everything the Father told me."

John 15:15 (NLT)

GOD SAYS

Do you know what it feels like to be redeemed and justified? When Christ took our sins for us, when he was brutally beaten for us, we were redeemed. His bloodshed saved us, now we are free!

I AM REDEEMED!

"Yet God, in his grace, freely makes us right in his sight. He did this through Christ Jesus when he freed us from the penalty for our sins."

Romans 3:24 (NLT)

GOD SAYS

Have you ever been a slave to anything? Do you remember the crippling feeling? With Christ, he has broken those chains and now you have victory in ALL THINGS!

I AM NO LONGER A SLAVE TO SIN, FOR I AM A CHILD OF GOD!

"We know that our old sinful selves were crucified with Christ so that sin might lose its power in our lives. We are no longer slaves to sin."

Romans 6:6 (NLT)

GOD SAYS

Has anyone ever held your past against you? Have they reminded you of what you've done? Even made feel guilty? In Christ, he has taken your guilty verdict.

I AM NOT CONDEMNED!

"So now there is no condemnation for those who belong to Christ Jesus."

Romans 8:1 (NLT)

GOD SAYS

Take a deep breath, Ready? Inhale, 1.2.3.4, now exhale 1,2,3,4! That's what freedom from the law of sin and death feels like. Embrace it!

DEATH COULD NOT HOLD HIM, DEATH CAN NOT HOLD ME!

"And because you belong to him, the power of the life-giving spirit has freed you from the power of sin that leads to death".

Romans 8:2 (NLT)

GOD SAYS

Some of us may have grew up without a parent, or both. The burden of the unknown may have even kept you bound. Who am I? Where do I come from? In Christ, he has adopted us into the Kingdom. Now, we are heirs of God. We no longer have to carry any burden because he has taken our suffering for us.

**I AM A CHILD OF THE
KING OF KINGS!**

"As a child of God, I am a fellow heir with Christ. And if children, then heirs (namely, heirs of God and also fellow heirs with Christ)– if indeed we suffer with him so we may also be glorified with him."

Romans 8:17 (NLT)

GOD SAYS

Have you ever felt rejected? Just wanted to be accepted and received by someone? In Christ, you have been received and accepted. Remember, he left the 99 for the one, you!

I AM ACCEPTED!

"I have been accepted by Christ. Receive one another, then, just as Christ also recieved you, to God's glory."

Romans 15:7 (NLT)

GOD SAYS

Imagine living in a world where there is complete darkness. Now, imagine you are the very light that the world needs to see. God calls us the salt and the light of the world.. With salt, it gives your food flavor, with light you help others see. Be the flavor of God that the world needs and the light in the darkness that we are surrounded by.

I AM THE LIGHT OF THE WORLD!

"You are the salt of the earth. But what good is salt of it has lost it's flavor? Can you make it salty again? It will be thrown out and trampled underfoot as worthless. You are the light of the world- like a city on a hilltop that cannot be hidden. No one lights a lamp and then puts it under a basket. Instead, a lamp is placed on a stand, where it gives light to everyone in the house.

GOD SAYS

Matthew 5:13-16 (NLT)

I don't know about you, but I have not always felt complete. I use to feel that something was missing in me. When I gave my life to Christ, it was then that I realized who I was and the authority that he has given me. Now, I am complete because my father is with me.

i <u>AM COMPLETE IN CHRIST!</u>

"So you are complete through your union with Christ, who is the head over every ruler and authority."

Colossians 2:10 (NLT)

GOD SAYS

Has anyone ever tried to label you? Even after you've changed, they would continue to tell you who you are? When you become a child of Christ, you are also crucified with him. The good news is we now live by faith. The life that we now live is no longer our own, but he who lives within us.

CHRIST LIVES IN ME!

"My old self has been crucified with Christ. It is no longer I who live, but Christ lives in me. So I live in this earthly body by trusting in the Son of God, who loved me and gave himself for me."

Galatians 2:20 (NLT)

GOD SAYS

Good news! You are a winner. You have the V I C T O R Y! Give thanks to God that with every trial, test, through every storm you may endure, you will have Victory!

I AM VICTORIOUS!

"But thank God! He gives us victory over sin and death through our Lord Jesus Christ."

1 Corinthians 15:57 (NLT)

GOD SAYS

This year has been one of many test, many trials, and many situations outside of my control. Through them all, I had peace. Initially, I was confused for a brief moment because of my lack of understanding. "How can I have peace when all hell is breaking loose, literally". Then God reminded me that HE gives me peace that surpasses what I can understand.

I AM GUARDED BY GOD'S PEACE!

"Then you will experience God's peace, which exceeds anything we can understand. His peace will guard your hearts and minds as you live in Christ Jesus."

Philippians 4:7 (NLT)

GOD SAYS

Have you ever created something? Maybe you went to a potter class and turned clay into a cup, or a vase. Designed a outfit and sewed it to life? Built something and saw the end result of it? We are God's workmanship, his finished product. As his finished product, we are to complete his work that he has predestined for us before the foundations of the earth were formed.

I AM GOD'S WORKMANSHIP!

"For we are his workmanship, created in Christ Jesus unto good works, which God hath before ordained that we should walk in them."

Ephesians 2:10 (KJV)

GOD SAYS

What does it mean to honor your body? How do you honor your body? Because the Spirit of God is within you, you're to remain holy. The word *honor* means to respect highly. Therefore, we are to respect our bodies highly, and to a higher standard. not just because we have the Spirit of God, but because Christ has paid the ultimate price for us.

I AM GOD'S TEMPLE!

"I am a branch of the true vine, and a conduct of Christ's life. I am the true vine and my Father is the gardener. I am the vine; you are the branches. The one who remains in me--and I in him--bears much fruit, because apart from me you can accomplish nothing."

John 15:1, 5 (NLT)

GOD SAYS

Christ is such a just God that he took the punishment that was intended for us. He took the penalty that would have separated us from him because he loves us. I mean Truly loves us! Because he took what was owed to us, we are now righteous.

I AM <u>THE RIGHTEOUSNESS OF</u> GOD!

"For he hath made him to be sin for us, who knew no sin; that we might be made the righteousness of God in him."

2 Corinthians 5:21 (KJV)

GOD SAYS

Do you know what it means to be more than a conqueror? It means to win. I win, we win! I know that I continue to reiterate that God loves us, but I have to say it again. God loves us more than anyone else and gave us the winning title in every battle!

I AM <u>MORE THAN A CONQUEROR</u>!

"Nay, in all these things we are more than conquerors through him that loved us.

Romans 8:37 (KJV)

GOD SAYS

I am set apart. My God knew me before my mother and set me apart for a time such as this. He knows my name and the amount of hairs on my head. Who wouldn't serve a God like this?

I AM SET APART!

"I knew you before I formed you in your mother's womb. Before you were born I set you apart and appointed you as my prophet to the nations."

Jeremiah 1:5 (NLT)

GOD SAYS

Why worry when the Lord supplies ALL your needs according to his riches and glory? I don't care how impossible your need may be, my God is a promise keeper. If you continue to have faith and trust in God, you will see all your needs be supplied.

I AM KEPT BY GOD!

"And this same God who takes care of me will supply all your needs from his glorious riches, which have been given to us in Christ Jesus.

Philippians 4:19 (NLT)

GOD SAYS

Take a moment and look in the mirror. Tell yourself, "I am fearfully and wonderfully made!" Remind yourself who you are and whom you belong to. God took his time creating you to his desire. Whenever you look at yourself and don't feel "*enough*", remind yourself that your Father makes no mistakes.

I AM FEARFULLY AND WONDERFULLY MADE!

"For thou hast possessed my reins: thou hast covered me in my mother's womb. I will praise thee; for I am fearfully and wonderfully made; marvellous are thy works; and that my soul knoweth right well.

Psalm 139:13-15 (KJV)

GOD SAYS

Let us make man in our image. Wow! God thought we were worthy enough to be made in His image. Doesn't that make you want to represent him well? I am created by the creator in his image. Take a moment and let that sink in.

I WAS CREATED IN GOD'S IMAGE!

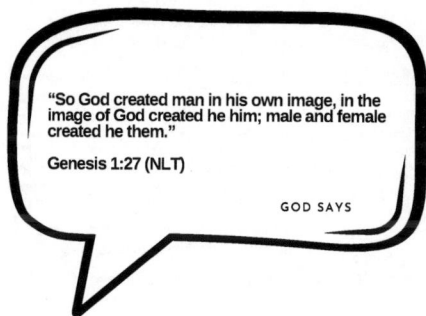

"So God created man in his own image, in the image of God created he him; male and female created he them."

Genesis 1:27 (NLT)

GOD SAYS

How does it make you feel when your lover calls you beautiful? How do you feel inside? What does being in their presence feel like? How does it feel when they continuously call you beautiful? That is the same feeling I get with Christ. It reminds me of a school girl. What is it that we would say? "You really think I am beautiful?" Want to know what's even better than that? He actually means it!

I AM BEAUTIFUL!

"You are altogether beautiful, my darling, beautiful in every way."

Song of Solomon 4:7 (NLT)

GOD SAYS

Just like any other loving parent, there are guidelines that we must abide by. If we obey, and keep our Father's covenant, we will be his treasured possession. It seems so simple right? Follow these rules and you'l forever be his special possession. Anytime someone considers you special, or their treasure, you can always count on them showering you with all kinds of possessions! Christ is no different.

I AM GOD'S SPECIAL POSSESSION!

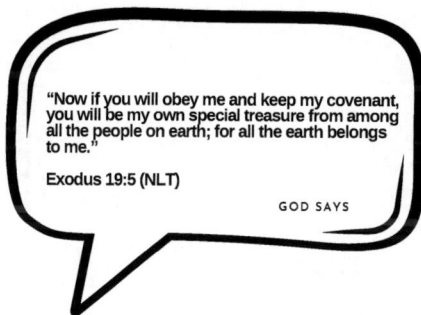

"Now if you will obey me and keep my covenant, you will be my own special treasure from among all the people on earth; for all the earth belongs to me."

Exodus 19:5 (NLT)

GOD SAYS

We all want to be understood by someone. Whenever we converse with someone and tell them how we are feelings, we want them to listen and also *understand*. In Christ, he does! He understands. I love that I don't have to over explain with him because he gets me!

I AM UNDERSTOOD BY GOD!

"O Lord, you have examined my heart and know everything about me."

Psalms 139:1 (NLT)

GOD SAYS

I am precious in the sight of the Lord. He sees me and because of his love for me, he will handle all of my afflictions.

I AM SEEN PRECIOUS!

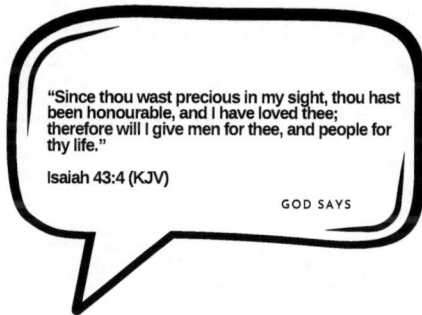

"Since thou wast precious in my sight, thou hast been honourable, and I have loved thee; therefore will I give men for thee, and people for thy life."

Isaiah 43:4 (KJV)

GOD SAYS

By his stripes I am healed. He was bruised so that I can be healed. My God has healed me from physical and spiritual wounds. How can I not serve my Lord knowing that I no longer have to suffer?

I AM HEALED!

"O Lord my God, I cried unto thee and thou hast healed me."

Psalms 30:2 (KJV)

GOD SAYS

I have the joy of the Lord down in my heart. Imagine
going through life lessons, and you feel joy instead of
anger, or pain. In Christ, the joy from the Lord is
promised to us.

I AM JOYFUL!

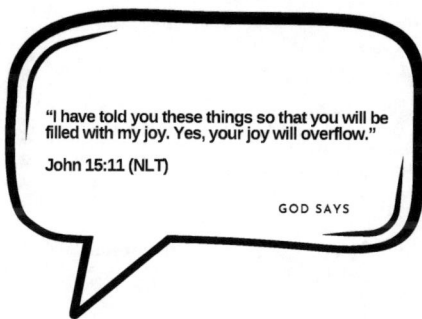

"I have told you these things so that you will be
filled with my joy. Yes, your joy will overflow."

John 15:11 (NLT)

GOD SAYS

When we become citizens of Christ. All things that tied us to our past is gone. We become a new creation and have no ties to our old life. A lot of times, shame tries to cripple us, or tell us who we still are, but through Christ, we no longer live by those old ways and desires.

<u>I AM A NEW CREATION!</u>

"This means that anyone who belongs to Christ has become a new person. The old life is gone; a new life has begun!

2 Corinthians 5:17 (NLT)

GOD SAYS

When you hear the word strong, your mind tends think of physical strength. Muscles, biceps, even a toned body. Strength from Christ comes from all life situations. No matter what you endure, you have strength that comes from the Lord. Once you learn that your strength doesn't come from the physical gym, but the gym in the spirit, you will have faith and know it is well.

_____ I AM STRONG! _____

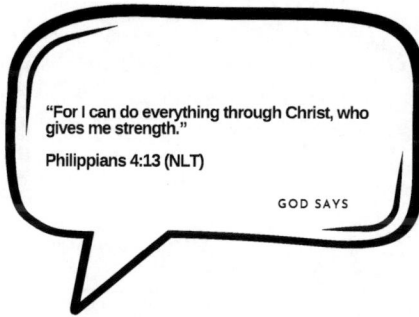

"For I can do everything through Christ, who gives me strength."

Philippians 4:13 (NLT)

GOD SAYS

Rich in everything but money is something most don't won't/ can't fathom. I have obtained inheritance that those who are detached from Christ can't image. Inheritance to the world looks like fame, money, cars, and houses. In Christ, our inheritance is everlasting life with him. What's more rewarding than that?

_____ I AM RICH! _____

"Futhermore, because we are united with Christ, we have received an inheritance from God, for he chose us in advance, and he makes everything work out according to his plan."

Ephesians 1:11 (NLT)

GOD SAYS

When you tell someone you're blessed, the first thing they think of is the physical thing. I am blessed in my soul and in my opinion, that is greater than any physical thing God could grant me. I am blessed in good health, and peace in my mind. I have a healed soul and a minded heart. God has truly blessed me.

_____ **I AM BLESSED!** _____

"All praise to God, the father of our Lord Jesus Christ, who has blessed us with every spiritual blessing in the heavenly realms because we are united with Christ."

Ephesians 1:3 (NLT)

GOD SAYS

There's the world standard of wisdom, then there is God's standard of wisdom. His thoughts and ways are not ours. He has giving us wisdom, righteousness, and he has sanctified us. We can not have wisdom, righteousness or sanctification without Christ.

I AM SANCTIFIED!

"I am a branch of the true vine, and a conduct of Christ's life. I am the true vine and my Father is the gardener. I am the vine; you are the branches. The one who remains in me--and I in him--bears much fruit, because apart from me you can accomplish nothing."

John 15:1, 5 (NLT)   GOD SAYS

Many believe because we are breathing, we are alive. However, the word tells us that in order to live, we have to die to sin. (Romans 6:10) Sin is not to reign in our bodies anymore, but we are to obey the word of God. Sin separates us from Christ, but if we hope to live, we are to live right in Christ.

_____ I AM ALIVE. _____

"When he died, he died once to break the power of sin. But now that he lives, he lives for the glory of God. So you also should consider yourselves to be dead to the power of sin and alive to God through Christ Jesus. Do not let sin control the way you live; do not give in to sinful desires."

Romans 6:10-12 (NLT)

GOD SAYS

In the mist of all danger around me, because I fear the Lord, I am safe. Christ delivers me from the hand of the enemy who tried to take me out. I am safe because I have found refuge in God.

I AM SAFE!

"For the angel of the Lord is a guard; he surrounds and defends all who fear him. Taste and see that the Lord is good. Oh, the joys of those who take refuge in him!"

Psalms 34:7-8 (NLT)

GOD SAYS

Have you ever heard the saying, you become who you spend the most time with? When you spend countless amounts of hours in someone's presence, you tend to speak like them, finish their sentences and even look like them. When you spend time with Christ, it shows. You tend to look more like him than you do yourself. I am delighted to know that I am like Christ.

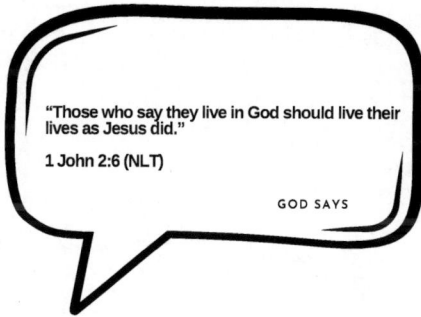

I AM LIKE CHRIST!

"Those who say they live in God should live their lives as Jesus did."

1 John 2:6 (NLT)

GOD SAYS

Have you ever wondered about salvation? Where would you go after death? What happens to your spirit/soul? In Christ, we are given *salvation* because there is no other way to live with God eternally, except through Christ!

_____ **I AM SAVED!** _____

"There is no salvation in no one else! God has given no other name under heaven by which we must be saved."

Acts 4:12 (NLT)

GOD SAYS

As an ambassador for Christ, (*high ranking diplomatic*) to represent him here on earth, I urge you to resign from your fleshy desires. I urge you to get right with Christ. For none of us know the time nor the hour when the Father will return. Remember it's never too late.

I AM AN AMBASSADOR FOR CHRIST! _____

"So we are Christ's ambassadors; God is making his appeal through us. We speak for Christ when we plead," "Come back to God"

2 Corinthians 5:20 (NLT)

GOD SAYS

When I think of God and his mercy, I am thankful for his compassion that he shows me. The kindness that endures in me, and the favor that I have received. His mercy surrounds me in all that I do.

I AM SURROUNDED BY
GOD'S MERCY!

"Many sorrows shall be to the wicked; but he who trusts in the Lord, mercy shall surround him."

Psalms 32:10 (NLT)

GOD SAYS

Of course I would end our journey with a four letter word that
has strategically been fighting to reinstate us back to our
original placement here on earth, *Love. "For God so loved the
world, that he gave his only son"* (John 3:16) God loves you and
I so much that he did all of this for us. I pray you are left full. I
pray that your identity in Christ is secure and you stand firm in
know who you are. "The Lord bless you and keep you; the Lord
make his face shine on you and be gracious toward you and
give you peace."
-Numbers 6:24-26 (NIV)

I AM LOVED!

"For God so loved the world, that he gave his
only begotten Son, that whosever believeth in
him should not perish, but have everlasting life."

John 3:16 (KJV)

GOD SAYS

Printed in Great Britain
by Amazon